Pigs

by Robin Nelson

first step nonfiction

Lerner Publications Company · Minneapolis

What lives on a farm?

Pigs live on a farm.

A female pig is a **sow**.

A male pig is a **boar**.

Pigs have a curly tail.

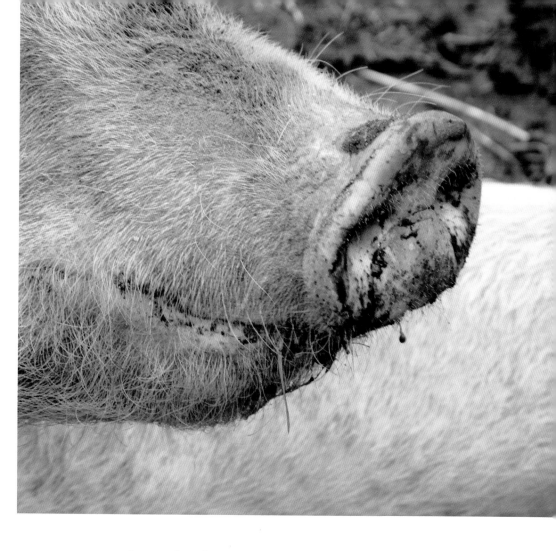

A pig's nose is called a **snout**.

Pigs have hair called bristles.

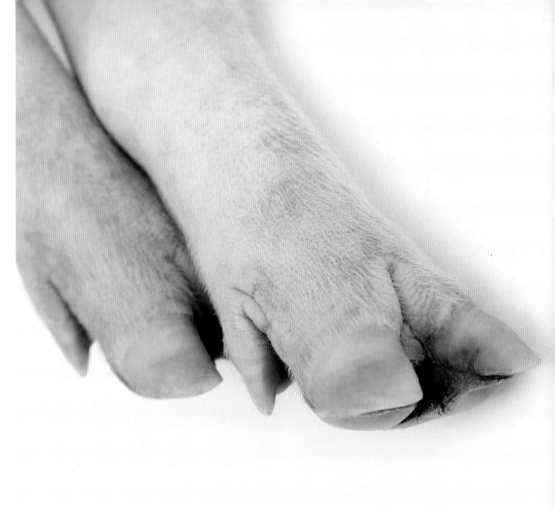

A pig's foot is called
a **hoof**.

Pigs eat vegetables, grains, and insects.

Pigs drink a lot of water.

A baby pig drinks its mother's milk.

A baby pig is called
a **piglet**.

Farmers keep pigs inside
a barn.

Pigs like to be outside too.

On hot days, pigs roll in
the mud to keep cool.

It is fun to see pigs on
the farm!

tail

ear

eye

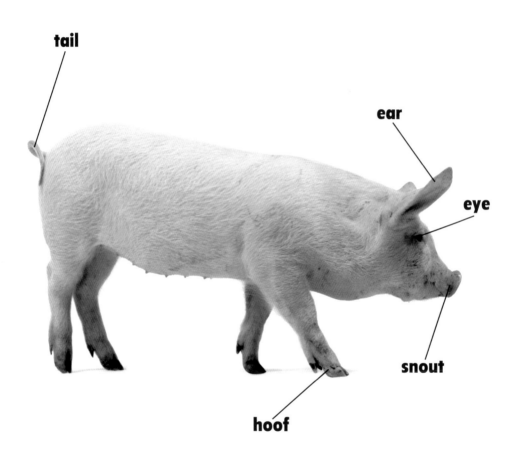

snout

hoof

Parts of a Pig

There are many different kinds of pigs. Pigs can be many different colors—pink, black, gray, and white. Piglets are soft and pink. Older pigs have rough hair on their skin called bristles.

Pig Facts

 A group of pigs is called a herd.

 Pigs are also called hogs or swine.

 Pigs cannot sweat.

 Barns keep pigs cool in the summer and warm in the winter.

Pigs cool off in the mud. Mud also protects them from insect bites and sunburn.

 Pork is a kind of meat we get from pigs. Bacon and ham come from pigs.

 Pigs can swim! They do the "dog paddle."

 Sows give birth to 6 to 12 piglets at a time.

Glossary

 boar – a male pig

 hoof – a pig's foot

 piglet – a baby pig

 snout – a pig's nose

 sow – a female pig

Index

The images in this book are used with the permission of: © iStockphoto.com/Gene Krebs, p. 2; © Larry Lefever/Grant Heilman Photography/Alamy, p. 3; © SuperStock, Inc./SuperStock, pp. 4, 6, 22 (bottom); © Monika Graff/Getty Images, pp. 5, 22 (top); © Karlene Schwartz, pp. 7, 11, 22 (second from bottom); © Royalty-Free/CORBIS, p. 8; © IMAGEMORE Co., Ltd./Imagemore/ Getty Images, pp. 9, 22 (second from top); © Cheryl Koralik/America 24-7/Getty Images, p. 10; © age fotostock/SuperStock, p. 12; © Scott Bauer/U.S. Department of Agriculture/Photo Researchers, Inc., pp. 13, 22 (middle); © Karen Kasmauski/CORBIS, p. 14; © iStockphoto.com/ tillsonburg, p. 15; AP Photo/University of Florida, Thomas Wright, p. 16; © Jeff Speed/First Light/Getty Images, p. 17; © Dorling Kindersley/Getty Images, p. 18. Front Cover: © Michael Krabs/imagebroker/Alamy

Lerner Publications Company
A division of Lerner Publishing Group, Inc.
241 First Avenue North
Minneapolis, MN 55401 U.S.A.

Website address: www.lernerbooks.com

Library of Congress Cataloging-in-Publication Data

Nelson, Robin, 1971–
    Pigs / by Robin Nelson.
       p.   cm. — (First step nonfiction. Farm animals)
    Includes index.
    ISBN 978-0-7613-4059-1 (lib. bdg. : alk. paper)
    1. Swine—Juvenile literature. I. Title.
    SF395.5.N45 2009
    636.4—dc22   2008024740

Manufactured in the United States of America
3 – DP – 3/1/10